GAZE BACK

MARYLYN TAN

GEORGIA REVIEW BOOKS
EDITED BY Gerald Maa

GAZE BACK

MARYLYN TAN

The University of Georgia Press

ATHENS

2022 paperback edition
by the University of Georgia Press
© 2018 by Marylyn Tan
Athens, Georgia 30602
www.ugapress.org
All rights reserved
Printed and bound by Sheridan Books, Inc.

The paper in this book meets the guidelines
for permanence and durability of the Committee on
Production Guidelines for Book Longevity of the
Council on Library Resources.

Most University of Georgia Press titles are
available from popular e-book vendors.

Printed in the United States of America

22 23 24 25 26 P 5 4 3 2 1

Library of Congress Cataloging-in-Publication Data

Names: Tan, Marylyn, 1993– author.
Title: Gaze back / Marylyn Tan.
Description: Athens, Georgia : The University of Georgia Press, 2022.
Identifiers: LCCN 2021043712 (print) | LCCN 2021043713 (ebook) |
ISBN 9780820362427 (paperback) | ISBN 9780820362410 (ebook)
Subjects: LCGFT: Poetry.
Classification: LCC PR9570.S53 T383 2022 (print) | LCC PR9570.S53 (ebook) |
DDC 821/.92—dc23/eng/20211020
LC record available at https://lccn.loc.gov/2021043712
LC ebook record available at https://lccn.loc.gov/2021043713

First published in the English language in Singapore
by Ethos Books, an imprint of Pagesetters Services Pte Ltd Singapore 573972
Copyright © 2018 by Marylyn Tan
All rights reserved

For Daddy and Mummy, for fearing for me,
and letting me do what I need to, all the same.

If you're unwilling to undress
don't enter into the stream of Truth.

—RŪMĪ

    sorry about the scene at
the bottom of the stairwell
        and how I
ruined everything by saying it out
loud.

—RICHARD SIKEN
Litany in Which Certain Things are Crossed Out

 the moon is not
a favor machine

—CAConrad
Width of a Witch

CONTENTS

NASI KANG KANG   11

BLADES NAMED DELILAH   19

BARRIER METHOD   25

BEDROOM NUDE COFFEE TABLE BOOK   27

SEXTS FROM THE UNIVERSE   35

CURSING THE FIG TREE   45

C:\Users\marylyn.tan\UnDocuments\Queer Bodies   55

UNICODE HEX   59

NASI KANG KANG

I asked the internet about nasi kang kang

google said:
some southeast asian cultures believe
that virginal fluids, including menstrual blood
have special supernatural powers
and is commonly used by individuals
and witch doctors in rituals

google said,
according to malay folklore
a woman who feeds her husband or
boyfriend with nasi kang kang
can have absolute control over him

kang kang means to straddle
squat, because you don't raise your leg to pee
queef, because you're claiming property
spread your thighs like a rumour   split
the red sea so   you can
keep your marriage together

like a shitty science experiment

take part in the water cycle
above a pot of fresh-cooked rice
let vapour condense at what
themalaysianlife.blogspot.sg calls
your muff

to rain upon the padi field
of your philips rice cooker

the idea is
witchcraft comes naturally
to women

but which
witch
women

okay, but then *hor*
my hubby say white rice too fattening *then how*

the caloric intake of nasi kang kang
is half that
of swallowing your pride

okay but then *hor*
I sometime forget to wash my down there
& sometime wash oreddi still very smiauly[1]
I scared my boyfriend eat already
recognise my chao chee bye[2]

the hot air rising from the cooker
got tightening effect on your lovehole
like brand new

so after the rice steam
his one will also cock *steam*[3]
he will stop calling your labia flaps
roast beef after you use your

pleasure cooker

okay, but then *hor*
nasi kang kang is fake one *then how*
I asked SGForum. they asked
ijit cai png[4]

---

1   A colloquial pronunciation of the word 'smelly'
2   (Lit.) 'smelly vagina'
3   (Colloq.) cock steam – 'erection'
4   Ijit – Chinese-Singlish pronunciation of 'is it'; cai png – 'rice with
assorted dishes'

they asked
steam rice where got kang kong?

I said sian you all multiracial society
machiam like don't know other cultures *sia*
like never eat lassi lomak until gelat before
so not boleh.[5] cannot make it one. like that
I ownself answer my own question

but then *hor*
everyday I work until damn late damn *cui*[6]
no time to cook no maid *how*????

themalaysianlife.blogspot.sg says:
for busy career women, useful
improvisations to this recipe include using
claypot chicken rice

just tar pau the rice
and do the kang kang at home

no need to keep a pet dog

5   machiam, lassi lomak and gelat are (predominantly Chinese) bastardisations of the Malay
words macam ("like; similarly to"), nasi lemak (lit. "fatty rice", a staple Malay dish) and jelak
(originally "bored" but has come to mean "cloyingly rich")
6   'wilted; tired'

just get a man

falling in love is a fistfight
it is common to hear bells
when you finally win the tinder match
some will tell you
there's not much difference between
a wrestling & a wedding ring

for many career women
there are pot lids like glass ceilings
over their rice bowls

watering their wetlands to make sure
they are wanted

these thighs were made for walking
not waterlogging

I had a vision of a woman
squatting over food
like she was exercising
her residential rights
to the kitchen

my mother had a fridge magnet that read
THE WOMAN WHO
BRINGS HOME THE BACON
SHOULDN'T HAVE TO COOK IT

but that's possible only after you
hire someone to make sure
the bacon cooks
itself

it doesn't matter
if your nasi kang kang is organically-sourced   vegan
& gluten-free

it's not the
emotionally-healthy option
keeping body & soul together is
much more than a campaign telling
GOOD GIRLS TO SWALLOW

instead of starving yourself

eat your own nasi kang kang
fall madly under your own spell

forget those who
call you demon for you are
self-possessed—

nobody needs a recipe to cook rice
instead, gardening tips:

weed out self-doubt
slash & burn those who
tell you to be both curved
& skinny as a sickle

pluck up every impulse to
sink claws into flab
& perish the thought
you are hungry

only to please

BLADES NAMED DELILAH

the evolved woman has
body in her hair but no
hair on her body

deforestation
must attend
civilisation

samson
give me strength
we're divesting   you of undergrowth

against the toilet sink mirrors
delilah maintains samson's undercut

tells her

sprinkle pubes
on those who talk shit
about them

samson never shaves her underarms
practised political move

NO SHAVE NOVEMBER
as pragmatic manoeuvre:

in the event she falls prey
to the lang suir
there will be ample hair
to stuff into the back
of her neck

how dare
you have follicles

lang suir trims her nostrils
an act of submission
lays each clipping
at your feet

inhales them with the dust
as part of good housekeeping

women who don't shave:
PRCs, HOMOSEXUALS
UGLIES

NO SHAVE NOVEMBER
as grandiose gesture:
beard culture
magnificence or sideshow

depends on
who's under the tent

it's very simple
        you pay the stranger
                wax congeals on your flesh
they tear out
        your pain by the roots

one brazilian is enough

to make three excellent
voodoo effigies

girls being pixie
gobbling in their bedrooms
each stray hair clumping
on their tongues   tensile strands
clinging to saliva
gleaning each corner
spool of nylon dreads

each hacking swallow
human furball

a story where she
goes to hospital
& they find
a rat-king of knots in her
                        stomach

was so nervous
fingernails wouldn't
do

one night she wakes
choking frangipani
looking back at staring eyelessness
cold clutching the ceiling
the lengths draping
gingerly her face just so

so

            that's
            why
                        she's been finding
            all those long black strands
            in their bed

all she thinks is,

    there's still time

    to cancel the appointment

    with the private eye

NO SHAVE NOVEMBER
no sex November
for some

for 1.50
a pair of tweezers may be procured

no excuses
are valid

 "these hairs I'm keeping,
I made them *myself*

with food that I *paid for*"

For excipients, see 6.1.* →	when they are addicted [...], they are under control of →	the Medicinal Product MERCILON →	parsley steeped in hot water makes abortion tea but that was coriander →	4.2.2. How to start taking Mercilon →
	got no railing. so you don't know where the danger is. ↑			
		your birthday spent looking for someone to sell you Plan B ↓	If the user is less than 12 hours late in taking any tablet, ↓	very fast. ↓
to attain adequate suppression ↑	two tubes of Vitamin C will do it, (she said) taught a Thai girl got it cheap from Mustafa			
	if not, you need to walk very carefully. ↓			

Barrier Method (center)

every day 1 per day take at the same time →	Starting [...] is allowed →	in relation ships you must →
	experience breakthrough bleeding →	
	have boundaries →	
if got railing, you can run up & down ↓	relationship with boundary is like staircase with railing. ↓	a barrier method is recommended ↓

Words in Adobe Garamond Pro taken from information slip within Mercilon package.

25

BEDROOM NUDE COFFEE TABLE BOOK

slight filipino man with a chunky   *camera*   *introduces him as performative*
signalling photographer
flicks through shots
of my friend naked in starbucks:

"I HAVE ANOTHER PROJECT—

what people are into:
the raw portrayal of raw girls being unguarded & raw

apply words liberally
candid & *vulnerable* jostling
bloodied slabs on a block   candied sweetmeat

carefully laid
to catch the light

maybe five seconds
before the flies descend
again

the tropics
you know

this one take picture *swee*
but / of-course cannot be fat *lah*
fat / still got people want *meh*

[photo: subject
mostly on her knees in the confessional
with the red light on

sliding her money into that space
between tampon & switchblade letting
rosary beads swarm the wood
grain thwarting
her fingers down her
throat to fish out
bolita ball bearings below her skin

the weight of which is imaginary
& unbearable]

    "TO BE HONEST WITH YOU
    I'M NOT REALLY INTERESTED
    IN ALL OF THAT POLITICAL STUFF
    I JUST WANT TO GET MY ART
    ON A WALL

[photo: stray delilah hairs
littered below
the bed. an overeager moult

tattered cuticles sting because
a healthy vagina's pH is
less than 4.5

an acidity
between
orange juice & beer]

      face must okay-*one*, got boops
      hair a bit messy-messy, neh *cheng kor* [1]
      lighting must romantic a bit pose
      machiam natural
      get chinese better
      mixed-race more better.
      but don't get those eurasian one look like indian

      later *sekali* nobody want to buy

---

1   *neh* – truncated form of 'never'; *cheng kor* – lit. 'wear[ing] pants or trousers': not wearing bottoms

[photo: a girl with soft high breasts & short hair
quirky not too butchy
belly red-lined a wrinkle
from slouching too much one nipple
erect & the other squinting creased
at the camera
lips drawn back uneven
unbrushed teeth]

    "EUROPEANS REALLY LIKE LOOKING AT
    ASIAN GIRLS, NAKED,
    THINGS LIKE THAT, IN THEIR BEDROOMS
    DOING EVERYDAY THINGS
    I'M DOING A SERIES OF THOSE GIRLS
    IN A COFFEE TABLE BOOK

[photo: a jawless girl
sprawled crumple-skinned parquet
in the hours where no one knocks
looking up online curses
for exes involved with
yeast infections &
lesbian bed death

candid *candida*]

"I'M TELLING YOU THIS IN SECRET
DON'T TELL ANYONE!

all these girls come in
think they damn big
think their pussy made of gold like that
at-the-end-of-the-day
they still using their body
to make money-what

[photo: subject hanging
over bedside dangles snot-veined bubbles
to wastebasket

deftly sucks mucus rope back
past valved membranes
slam-dunks snot residue
cramming phlegm gristles
flat-tongued against palate roof

sweet sick khaki wetland]

"I WANT IT TO BE A SURPRISE, BUT
EVENTUALLY I WANT THE GIRLS
TO TURN AROUND &
POINT THEIR MIDDLE FINGER TO THE CAMERA

[photo: a dislocating lotus position
like overboiled shrimp
the pestle of her flaking wart
wrapped contortionist
ankle pressed to cheek
gnawing epic dermis
off splayed toes

chews & swallows]

"LIKE A FUCK YOU TO SOCIETY!

[photo: close-up
a scalpful of blistering
barnacles minute shellfish
tunneled flesh holes
tonguing endlessly inside outside

turns you to open sores then
turns you to stone

the manicures for this nailment
scrabble up tarot crushing in
fist the emperor with the two of swords
paper beats rock
lighter beats paper
into talisman ash

gulping a whole glass]

    "BUT IT'S A SECRET."

[photo: a girl in her bedroom
keeps asking

what the fuck
I'm doing
what are you fucking
doing the fuck
do you think
you're doing]

SEXTS
FROM THE
UNIVERSE

DO NOT **KILL ME**
WITH YOUR **SHOES**

A printed A4-sized sign on paper in a transparent sleeve with pre-dominantly blue typeface and red font for emphasis inconsistently spaced, enlarged, and kerned, with a monochrome blue photograph image of a human eye, which seems to be of Caucasian ethnicity, edited to have a heart-shaped pupil leaking a stylized tear, as well as a footer photograph of blurred pink flowers tied to a tree trunk next to a pathway beside a busy intersection.

Bugis, Singapore, 2014

You will be surprized at dirts!

A green-edged white speech bubble on a glass-panelled shopfront of a Japanese lifestyle boutique display promoting a chemical product to make dental plaque in the oral cavity appear like black rubbings or soil.

Tokyu Hands, Orchard Central, Singapore, 2014

This entrance is not accessible to the disabled.

Sign at the entrance of a train station on a marble wall
leading to stairs descending with no lift or ramp in sight

Bras Basah, Singapore, 2016

KEEP LOVING ♥ IT WILL ALL WORK OUT

Handwritten script written in white correction fluid, all capitals, circling the topmost surface of a black public trash can.

Highgate, London, UK, 2015

FREEDOM
TO FUCK

A placard with freehand script, all capitals, in marker, held by a volunteer flanking an arch constructed from pink and white balloons.

Pink Dot, Singapore's largest annual LGBTQIA+ pride event, Hong Lim Park, Singapore, 2016

Please Slow Down
Thank You

An LED sign in the dark, which displays each time a
carpark barrier is raised.

Bencoolen Street, Singapore, 2016

CURSING THE FIG TREE:
THE HOLY PREPUCE & OTHER DELICIOUS RECIPES

1. *Crying and with compassion,*
    she began to think about

    the foreskin of Christ,
    where it may be located
    [after the Resurrection].

    And behold,
    soon she felt
    with the greatest sweetness
    on her tongue
    a little piece of skin alike
    the skin in an egg,

    which she swallowed. [1]

---

1 Wiethaus, Ulrike (2002). Agnes Blannbekin, Viennese Beguine: Life and Revelations.

2.   they call it fasting but time passes so slow   tasty christ.   pasty curly-
haired blue-eyed middle-eastern christ. women saints pickled in shrine sin gorge us swole
rolling eyes animals in tongues of flame panty cost   nailed to the cross nailed on the bed
        never find anyone else who burns so easy   joan of arc was
made of flesh   joan of arc was maid of orleans   we only barbecue the saints that
mean the most to us

turn the other cheek so fast
you get self-flagellating whiplash   kyrie e e ele e e i son   lord have mercy
✛ ALCHEMICAL SYMBOL FOR VINEGAR—THE JERUSALEM CROSS—beat me
gently with a hyssop stick—lift me to the martyred lips—the guilt an art form—
        the knees a penance—
        the pursed lips a furrowed heave church organ donors hollow within gutted
        indelible inedible incredible liturgical litany ritual rutting serpent gloaming egg gut
archly theological venial veal transgressions being

      WITH THE ASCENSION OF JESUS, ALL OF HIS BODY PARTS—EVEN
THOSE NO LONGER ATTACHED—ASCENDED WITH HIM

THE FORESKIN OF CHRIST WAS TRANSFORMED
      INTO THE RINGS
          OF SATURN[2]

---

2   Fabricius, Johann Albert (1728). *Bibliotheca Graeca (Vol. 14)* (in Latin). Hamburg. p. 17. *Adhuc ineditis praefixus Astericus*. Unpublished work.

3. *THIS IS MY BODY*

concept: a confessional box with a red light on / like an invitation / or a warning
concept: jesus as a teenaged girl. this is my body. this is my blood

in the beginning
the word was made flesh

jesus, taught the shame of a
sinful body, of a receptacle-like body, a true
vessel of christ. jesus being taught to keep his
legs closed

turns out
the chalice of the holy grail
is a menstrual cup

jesus christ
& the silicone goblet of fluids
jesus not being able to enter
the very temple where he preaches

jesus' mom telling him to
     GET RID OF THE BLOOD
with bared teeth &
barely-concealed disgust

jesus' schoolmates chanting

      PLUG IT UP, PLUG IT UP

in the girls' bathroom

throwing tampons at jesus

convinced they would fit

in the holes / in his hands & feet

the stigma of the stigmata

jesus doesn't have access to:

      the internet /   the feminine mystique /   the bleeding as power

         all he knows is potency /   transmuted into poison

fire /

     into filth

     the same day jesus learnt to cover his shame

     he figured out the Holy Prepuce of Christ

     meant jesus' foreskin

     the saviour's / private areas

        popularised / by the uncanonised

           Agnes Blannbekin's / holy visions

        enthusiastically transcribed

     by her confessor

a monk fascinated with
the body of christ

jesus pulls his robes a little tighter
doesn't want to be one of *those* prophets

at the last supper / subsisting on celery & water
this is my body   it is
beach ready. tonight we dine
but will throw it back up / roman catholic
vomitorium

because you always see a jacked christ but you never see a fat christ
the dadbod of christ / the kate moss waif-like figure of christ /
perpendicular stick thin christ

why were the faithful crying / at the eucharistic feast? because christ had
been a way fer so long   why were the faithful hungry at the eucharistic feast?
A LITTLE PIECE OF SKIN ALIKE THE SKIN IN AN EGG
communing in communion calorie count

it's one drink of vinegar / it's one piece of eggskin
it's one apple
for chrissakes
EAT ME

in the beginning
the word was made flesh
& some people say / that word was yes

this is my body, for public consumption
this is my body, salvation of swarming crowds

jesus has lost count of how many times
his ass has been stroked surreptitious back   of the hand
by the faceless faithful
            it's called backpalming because the fronts of your palms are pressed together in
penance

WHO   TOUCHED   ME

jesus said, (Luke 8:45)

who   touched me
again

jesus finds walking on water easier
than walking home alone at night
jesus walks with nails / clenched between his knuckles
if he didn't want to be crucified
he shouldn't have manifested in human form
if he didn't want us to tear it

he shouldn't have worn a one-piece seamless garment
he shouldn't have let the holy spirit in him
doesn't he know how many people
the holy spirit's been inside of?

maybe jesus still awakes dislodged some nights
the memory of thorns crowning his temples
& the only way he survives is by resurrecting the incident
but this time he controls / who flagellates him
whiplash trauma / requires exercise to heal /

jesus' safe space

is a tomb hewn in rock
a safeword like a great stone
rolling across his tongue
amen / amen / amen
amen /

amen

they nailed him to the cross with his legs closed
like a good girl /
like a good girl
jesus

crying silently in the garden of gethsemane
so as not to wake the others
allowing judas to kiss him / rather than resist him

jesus / still can be a Cool Girl if he wants

this is my body / take it & eat it
& never
ever
mention the blood

4. *In 1900, the Roman Catholic church ruled that anyone thenceforward writing or speaking of the Holy Prepuce would be excommunicated.*[3]

---

3   David Farley (2006). *Fore Shame*, Slate.com.

C:\Users\marylyn.tan\UnDocuments\Queer Bodies

LBTcircuit.py

queerfemalebody.py

ignore.py

freshmeet.txt

```
>>>open ("LBTcircuit.py")

potential_queer_lovers = ['Doc Martens Girl', 'Cute Bartender',
'Bleached Pompadour Dancing Alone', 'Unsure if Hipster or Lesbian',
'National Hockey Player', 'Gender Panic TA']

potential_queer_lovers.append('freshmeet.txt')

>>>open ("queerfemalebody.py")
if w in potential_queer_lovers:
     run rules_of_lesbian_attraction_SG


def rules_of_lesbian_attraction_SG:
     for item in (gender_presentation):
          if hair_length < 10cm:
       ]
               "MASC" = +1
          if hair_length >= 10cm:
               "MASC" = -1
          type(footwear):
               if ("boots", "brogues", "oxfords") = True:
                    "MASC" = +1
               if ("heels", "pumps", "wedges") = True:
                    "MASC" = -1
               if ("flip flops") = True:
                    "ATTRACTIVE" = -1
               else = True:
                    "UNCLASSIFIED" = +1
```

```
type (clothing):
        if ("binder", "too_tight_sports_bra",
        "button_down"):
                "MASC" = +1
        if ("cargo shorts"):
                "ATTRACTIVE" = -1


type(language):
        if "anglophone" = True:
                "EDUCATED".append()
        if "sinophone_local" = True:
                "HELICOPTER".append()
        if "sinophone_china" = True,
                "PRC".append()
        else:
                open("ignore.py")


type(colour):
        if "pale":
                "ATTRACTIVE" = +1
        else:
                "ATTRACTIVE" = -1
type(body):
calculate("freesize")
if "freesize" = True:
        "NORMAL_WEIGHT" = +1
else:
        "FAN_TONG" = +1
        append.FOOD_AS_SIN()
```

```
type (sexual_orientation):
    if "instances_contact_penis" < 1:
    "GOLD_STAR" = +1
     else:
        if "bisexual":
            "ATTRACTIVE" = -1
            "FICKLE-MINDED" = +1
            "LIKELY_TO-CHEAT" = +1
            "WILL_LEAVE_FOR_MAN" = +1
        if "trans_woman":
            if pre-op:
                "ANYTHING_BUT_PENIS" = -1,
                potential_queer_lovers.remove()
        if "trans man":
            "ANYTHING_BUT_PENIS" = +1
        else:
            lesbians_who_have_sex_with_men.append()
type (race):
if ("chinese"):
"ATTRACTIVE" = +1
  elif ("malay", "indian", "other"):
                open("educational_level_check.py",
                    "economic_prospect_check.py")


attraction_score = len("MASC" + "ATTRACTIVE" + "NORMAL_WEIGHT" +
"EDUCATED") / len(total)

if attraction_score > 0.5:
        open("allow_drinks_bought.py")
else:
    potential_queer_lovers.remove()
    for (random_excuse) in ("excuses").randomize():
    print (random_excuse)
```

UNICODE (HEX)

origin story

☿♐☿♍ λ

MADE THE WORLD AND NOW IT
WILL UNMAKE IT MADE THE
WORLD AND NOW IT WILL
UNMAKE IT MADE THE WORLD
AND NOW IT WILL UNMAKE

wheel ✿f dharma queen

tunnel boring gantry nailbite whittle worm-
eaten spine less grimoire sub text qwerty
word   was   made   infested
flesh   ingesting of   let   there
be   subsistence on light
communion wafer   investing
time-space bitcoin   eternity
        verm/acular the second   coming
creamy   cyberchurch   torrential
conscience file   corruption

I present you with

when I was twelve

my mother

do you read? they ask

gave me

this sadness to hold

and never asked for it

back

every card
in verse
mercurial release

HEX ED

A COMMON PROPERTY OF UNICODE
UNICODE IS COMMON PROPERTY
THE UNCONSCIOUS MIND SPEAKS IN SYMBOLS
PREVENT THOUGHT TO CIRCUMVENT RATIONALITY

Ritual to explicate each unicode (hex) symbol in everyday/extraordinary usage: Meditate on the lines of each unicode glyph by drawing and re-drawing it while repeating an idea or a phrase that befits it. Do this until the boundaries of meaning collapse and overlap. Then write down everything that occurs to you, pared down to a poem.

The following translingual symbols, most of which are found in the Unicode Standard, Version 8.0, appear over varied social and historical contexts. They are presented here with their descriptors, character codes, sets of free associations, and the poems they have spawned.

☽ ALCHEMICAL SYMBOL—FIRST QUARTER MOON
CHARACTER CODE: 0083 FROM: SYMBOL (HEX)
'SEXUAL INTERCOURSE AS INTERACTION RITUAL'

WAXES FAT / GOOD FOR COALESCING ENERGIES / FILLING EMERGENT / MOONCAKE CREAMPIE / LIST OF APPROVED INGREDIENTS / DIANA, GODDESS OF THE HUNT

silver gleaming spike hound makes   mud in your
uniqlo trousers   modern pants don't stand a chance
          foxbrush whisky flight   sunburnt & moaning
          forget all you knew   ladyfingers spent
sprouting croons cracking upart the dinner table with
their gestures   stop   my tiddlywinks my set-on-fire
drones my hunted cunts my A+-groans, you'll never
bottle me   screams the acrid   one who
makes you bleed

a pockmark & the gallows   a trusted
friend, on the piano, a tilted shadow in the   limp
mist

SYMBOL—INVERTED BLACK TRIANGLE
CHARACTER CODE: 25BC FROM: SYMBOL (HEX)
'PLEASURE AS INTRINSICALLY TIED TO GUILT'

▽ *THE WATER DROPLET / CHALICE / DOWNWARD FLOW / INTUITION / THE
UNCONSCIOUS MIND / GENERATIVE PROPERTIES OF THE WOMB*

▼ *WORK-SHY (ARBEITSSCHEU) / DISABILITY / ASOCIALITY / LESBIAN SOLIDARITY*

begin again, charming loach. fetishise the pythagorean march.
my slumbering horse molars grind on we're to cut your teeth
on high stakes. surrogate bliss. sentenced for heresy
by the macaques: tell the coffee cup your excuses
for pinkeye & languishing in bed / horrified
stockings & glances on trains only mean
you take up enough/correct/the right
amount of space. see: neon-lit
medusoids[1] whose whole
purpose is to love &
die in fibreglass:
each others'
sub sis
ten
ce

---

1   The term *medusa* was coined by Linnaeus in 1752 as a zoological name for jellyfish, alluding to
the tentacled head of Medusa in Greek mythology. Medusans or medusoids refer exclusively to the
non-polyp life-stage of those cnidarians, or jellyfish, corresponding to a pulsating gelatinous bell with
trailing tentacles.

ALCHEMICAL SYMBOL FOR GOLD / MASCULINE CHARIOT / CRYSTAL CHARGE / PINNACLE OF SPIRITUAL DEVELOPMENT / HAWK EYE GLARE / LIFE SURGE / BODY ELECTRIC / FACING EAST

windchime
with a resident spirit:

a cardinal screech from
my front yard when I used
to have a front yard

they're nesting in my
hurts again

misery
is priority

eating lemons
just a hobby

nosebleed parade in the stumble
slumber like a global-
warmed polar bear

       would resuscitate you but
I don't know how
the lips
will fall

the wildflower prince
only grows in the
temperature-controlled
glassdome Botanic
      (i.e.
      I gotta go see the cactuses

the cactuses
know what to do
with my succulent parts

ɵ ALCHEMICAL SYMBOL—SALT
CHARACTER CODE: 2C91 FROM: UNICODE (HEX)
'FOOD AS SIN'

*WARDING OFF / PROTECTIONS / DISSOLVING GASTROPODS / SEASONING AS NEEDED / THE
WAY TO A MAN'S HEART IS BETWEEN THE FOURTH AND FIFTH RIBS / FASTEN CONDOMS
OVER THRESHOLDS BEFORE INTIMACY AS PROTECTION*

no one takes you seriously
past the mutter of doorspring

the guilty burn & stutter

tiptoeing
past the siao zha bor[1]
with the filthy Clorox-fecal-water flung
dripping

from the ceiling

I'm ghosting out
again the washed flood
corridor

slick concrete
foam flipflop

trying not to look
the hole in her pants
in the eye

---

1   *siao zha bor*: colloquial Hokkien, derogatory phrase. Lit. 'crazy woman'.

ALL / NOTHING / EXISTING WITHIN LIMINAL SPACE / TO CASTRATE OR SPAY / THE
NOBILITY OF IMPARTIALITY / A LATIN ADJECTIVE MEANING 'NEITHER'

☿ ALCHEMICAL SYMBOL—GENDER DEVIANT
⚲ ALCHEMICAL SYMBOL—GENDER DEVIANT LYING ON ITS SIDE

salt will not cure
this nullness

A REAL BOY
WASHED UP
ON SHORE:

I was the first
to call you
'he'

spent the seaside
on nothing but
a *pondok* memory

summer salt
keeps the daemons
out

wrangled butterfly
tycoons

lower-lipped
banana

a blindfold
licks feelering
itself in the shade

shave your jointed
legs

to shave you
from yourself

☿ ALCHEMICAL SYMBOL—MERCURY
CHARACTER CODE: 263F FROM: UNICODE (HEX)

*QUICKSILVER / COMMUNICATION / OUROBOROS THE TAIL-SWALLOWER / A SUBSTANCE
PERMEATING ALL MATTER / CONTINUOUS RENEWAL / INDICATIONS OF BOTANICAL
HERMAPHRODITISM / A RALLYING SYMBOL OF INTERSEXEDNESS / VIOLENT
MISCOMMUNICATIONS IN RETROGRADE*

ingestion may lead to

inability to produce speech

& other acts

ALCHEMICAL SYMBOL—URINE
'CHARACTER CODE: 2680 FROM: UNICODE (HEX)'
'YOUR PEACE IS YOUR POWER'

*SQUARED DOT OPERATOR / SEXUAL FLUID SUBSTITUTE / LOVE SPELLS / LUCKY FEMALE
PISS FOR MOJO / UNJINXING EASY AS PASSING WATER INTO A RUNNING RIVER*

pissing
wars

never saw
a scissors so deep

plastic tied-wire
bloody bags in heat

backstage &
nowhere to go:

your tender spine
against the corkboard.

got the bartholomew goat[1].
got the slippered champagne.

just so you know
I'm a mere

heeled hoof
in sequins.

get my lungs;
yammer about how they taste so tasty
grilled over low heat.

---

1   A bartholomew goat is a method of preparing mutton with the goat having been
flayed alive and crucified upside-down, that is, headfirst towards the dinner table.

ALCHEMICAL SYMBOL—THUNDERSTORM
CHARACTER CODE: 2608 FROM: UNICODE (HEX)
'JUST BECAUSE YOU'RE HAVING FUN DOESN'T MEAN YOU'RE NOT ALL GOING TO DIE'

*RAGE-CLEANSING / LIGHTNING AS DESTROYER / IF YOU ARE NOT PART OF THE
SOLUTION YOU ARE PART OF THE PRECIPITATE / NO FLASH FLOOD PHOTOGRAPHY*

cold-pressed nose
palms splayed

I regret the fact of my legs.

I never wanted to be a cockatoo,
sulphur-clipped agent of hell,

just a tropical boy with talons

a spark in my father's eye
guilt & passion
(he is catholic)

I liked kneeling on a pedestal
because it was a break
from standing straight

never knew warmth?
not true

the way incense settles
in the lower lip
of my eye

ASTROLOGICAL SYMBOL—BLACK MOON LILITH
CHARACTER CODE: 26B8 FROM: UNICODE (HEX)

EMPTY FOCUS OF ECLIPSE DESCRIBED BY ORBIT / FIRST WIFE OF ADAM / FERTILE
CHAOS / THE INCARNATION OF LUST / CHILD-KILLING WITCH / EMBODIMENT OF
DESTRUCTION / NIGHT HAG SCREECH OWL / LILITH OF THE LONG HAIR / ENTRANCE OF
WOMEN THROUGH MIRRORS / FILTH
'SCROUNGED FROM THE SAME DIRT WE ARE THUS EQUAL' [1]

polyps bundled
ignoble sticks
for use as switches
mutton antlers
caught in a matrilineal
matrix   grid   codebreaker
river styx
syntax error

switch-identified hags
love to be on top

a time of beckoning:
crook your fingernail
throughwards
his pisshole

sounding (screech) renders
dial-up obsolete
python strangler
rogue programmer

---

1   Based on Lilith's creation myth, from Genesis 2:18, which some translations leave
out. Lilith, who was created before Eve, refused to acknowledge or allow the first man
Adam's superiority over her 'inasmuch as [they] were both created from the same soil'.
Because of this struggle for power, Lilith escaped and declined to return, becoming
instead a scourge on newborns, as well as a mother of demons.

aching breastclamps
do nothing to filter out yr
clumped dirt grunts

vacuum cleaner reprises
he will crush your head
and you will strike his heel[2]
       (dust-biter)

pregnant pause:
new-borne demons go through a
seething phase
sooth eruption

2   Genesis 3:15 New International Version (NIV) Bible

))ȣɼ♀♇ λ⊕ ▼ ▽ ☉ ⊖ ♀♁° □ɼ⎩☾
re: origin story / ARCHETYPAL EVIL

Turritopsis dohrnii medusa
biologically immortal
a back-and-forth *pls revert*　　　of two-stage cnidarian cycles
salted crystalline polyp　　　came unstuck in time

sometimes I shut myself　　　& think of my ah kong[1]
appearing as a crinkled ginko / pink fleshed foetus nut

I fall in love with girls / I can readily call daddy / not my real dad
descending father figure
　　　　　　　　figuratively / I have grand daddy issues

last time I saw ah kong he was

a spongy concave　　　skull fragment
save the biggest shards for last
crown the dust in stubborn urn

　　　crematorium blocks
　　　as public housing

　　　evoke ideographs
　　　as impending offering

1　*Ah kong* 'Grandfather' in Teochew or Hokkien

in the beginning,
man made goddess

an archetype made flesh implies the super
                             & sub human

about my grandfather:
he sang about bananas
                 he had testicles

     (changing for prayer night
     he turns away rather than turn
     the kids out of his room)

the childish certainty of
guys have one Thing
    (defied)
         girls have None
         (defined)

I LIKE BANANAS, BECAUSE THEY HAVE NO BONES
I DON'T LIKE PEACHES, BECAUSE THEY HAVE A STONE[2]

IN-REAL-LIFE USAGE / IMPLIES MEATSPACE WITH THIGHS
HYGIENE FEMININE / A SLIPPERY CLEANSED THING
THIS WORK IS FILTH-RICH / FLUIDS UNRELENTING

---

2   Lyrics of a song my grandfather used to sing while he ate bananas, circa approx. 2000-5

each
woman body
termed 'receptacle'

all my butches love me
all my all my butches love me
cohabiting / is a commitment to sheets / vessels shrilling / & covered in:

(glyphs)

chilli sauce / blue dye / snake sheddings / pesticides
wig hair / weapons / cough drops / adhesives
legal additives & preservatives
memory foam / state-sanctioned skin

wrung out, some days, unsmiling, that's all you
after that time we spent making it on the sand
lips untouched by ant or man
your skin a callus
drooling sores said
'my nose is rotting off'

scientifically-documented trigger for herpes simplex virus-1:
the ultraviolet light
in direct sun

a clear instruction:
just-enough solar power
this is how to make
      a wretch / a simpering traveller / a fingersmithing heist

        in a past life you were a—

         one night your parents awoke & turned off the air-conditioning, causing you
         to kick up your feet & scream bloody—

           all the ones you mistook for lesbians & the ones you thought couldn't
           be lesbians the daggers & the saints the goddamn Piscean
           sentimentalists the bitches the butch bois who believed
           they were unlovable wracking themselves gasping de-finned
           hitting bloat bottom gargled
           hiccup crushes & ace bandages
           will flatten you   barely breathing

clear as instruction:
      the warped sense of urine
          in a flushed sodium alley
choking your breast cuts
surfeit   meat counterfeit

when you come / seeking supplement

I maintain
your 'breasts' are a chest—
your 'clit' is a cock—
no matter what—

you're *good at catering to male ego*
    hard to swallow

found a fishbone
kibble spine
cat idol aspect
plastered velcro septic tongue

girls passing notes in made-up script / throat & teeth cannot produce / past the
alveolar ridge / the event horizon / fishhooks like finished lines / the universe
a mouthful / symptoms of rectal inadequacy / gravity's intestinal collapse /
imploding offering / offal prolapse
the retentive / un / productive
                indestructive

waste   not

keep the seeping sun / in a cool dry place

    the magi
            have been seeking you
            an eternity

AUTHOR'S NOTE

GAZE BACK arose, most simply, from distress. This particular work of writing was borne out of disgust, loathing, disillusionment, and a certain embodied fatigue of being hyper-scrutinised, by the self and society, that is perhaps intrinsic to the contemporary female experience.

In GAZE BACK, I take a particular interest in how best to represent the disenfranchised voices that speak to me the most. I was concerned with how to give not only voice, but shape and depth, to subaltern representations of minority gender, of race, of sexuality, while still remaining cognizant of my own principle positions of relative privilege in terms of finances, racial dynamics, and cisgender identity as a person and writer. More specifically, in fantasising an audience, I found myself wanting to write for the parts of me that felt they were discovered too late, recognised too late, embraced too late.

I wanted to write for a female, Singaporean, fatigued audience, who might be sexually deviant, who was perhaps a sexual minority but in no way less valuable as a person—an audience that understands being cast out, the sorrow of the 'shame of a / sinful body, of a receptacle-like body, a true / vessel' [1], the disillusionment with institutions and organised religion.

The answer to how to erect and carve out autonomous zones, whether temporary or not, is one I hope to obtain with this work. My thematic concerns centre on those who refuse to be 'decent' women, that is, those who cannot be law-abiding, god-fearing, mothers, daughters, wives, virgins, nuns, those who have neither temperance nor mercy, who put their pleasure before that of others'. In linking the feminine to the deviant, or rather, more closely scrutinising an intrinsic association that cannot divorce one from the other, I am also thinking about other forms of unconventional sexual practices, such as sexual kink, fetish-play, and BDSM.

Kink (when practised correctly and safely) is often brought up as an exemplar of a feminist space in which women are able to access sexual agency in being able to dictate their preferences and experiences. This is a natural extension of the self-mastery that comes with knowledge of the self—hence, the exhortation to *eat your own nasi kang kang* (NASI KANG KANG, pg 16). It is important to note also that none of these spaces exist in a strict binary or vacuum: for instance, most mainstream portrayals of kink serve to perpetuate hegemonic—and tired—narratives of male domination and female submission.

---

1   'CURSING THE FIG TREE', pg 45

The larger destination I started with in mind, therefore, was centred on the various ways in which femininity is policed, and in counterpoint to that, how one can liberate oneself from the validation presented in reward to the ideal feminine form and performance required of us by ourselves and the larger paradigms within which we work.

What are the ramifications of the alienation and othering of minority experiences? How can we break away from the default positionality of 'white cisgender maleness' that so often informs how we consume and interpret poetry, art, and all communication? And in the process of being complicit with or tearing apart from systems of brutal efficiency, where is the individual driven? In what spaces can the subaltern exist wholly and utterly as themselves, especially and even within a dominant, consensual concept of reality? Finally, how can we rise above and derive power from existing hegemony that others and places minorities in positions of disadvantage?

Representation of subaltern voices has little meaning to me if it does not strive for resolution or breakthrough. What further effects does existing in a marginal position have on feminine access to power and resources? Working on the assumption that the occult serves as a means of rising from restrictions both structural and individual, the trans-genre work aims to explore—and decimate—the boundaries between forms and subjects.

In the book, I utilise witchcraft and occult (literally, 'unknown') technologies as a vehicle to explore new ways of manifesting the embodied, esoteric desires of the self, whether because or in spite of the systems of hierarchy we are made to operate within.

Occult principles are useful for thinking about sexual and gender trouble, and indeed about power dynamics. So much of why witchcraft is vilified is the same reason it is empowering—one of the earliest quotes I encountered in my occult studies, and one of my most beloved, its source now lost to time, reads: 'The secret of magic is, any fool can do it.' What a threat to established orders, to institutions of power, that anyone could bypass the emissaries of the gods and attain transcendence for themselves!

☽

GAZE BACK presents re-imaginings of the feminine ideal, elaborated in the idea of gender minorities existing freely only within spaces marked as taboo. The archetype of the empowered woman is so often seen in patriarchal culture and entertainment as occult, sexually 'deviant', or only in markedly 'feminine' or matriarchal spaces. We are allowed our powerful witch crones, but only as villains. Women free from male control are generally failures of femininity in various ways: they are sexually promiscuous, predatory or plain undesirable. I was fascinated by the idea of the feminine grotesque as power. Is male desire disempowering?

Can autonomy be regained by the ugly, the dreadful, and the strange woman?

The occult, for me, provides a rejection, or at least a counterpoint, to tradition and orthodoxy that frequently incorporates the historic marginalisation and submission of women. In this manner the avenue of witchcraft is utilised as a way for women to create paths towards agency and power in a patriarchy where men monopolise access to most of the resources. Working with the idea of the immaterial (that is, the intuitive, unpredictable, subconscious, emotional, illogical) as the domain of women serves once again to make femaleness the Other. In addition, immateriality dictates that it is so often only within the realm of the metaphysical or religious that a feminine presence commands respect, fear, or authority.

Thus I felt an exploration of the occult, especially practices indigenous to Southeast Asia and Singapore, and in particular practices of personal significance as empowering, was due. Let us look to the pantheons of goddesses (perhaps only respected because of the 'mother' role they play), to the limited respect afforded to the soothsayers, witches, high priestesses, hijra, healers, and mediums.

☾

I struggled very much with making the book 'worth the audience's while', which really meant, making it worth my own while. While negotiating the ever-present spectre of the audience's gaze, I learnt to play with the dynamic tension of the author-reader relationship, and walk the tightrope between challenging the reader and creating pleasure for them. Furthermore, in keeping with the zeitgeist of identity politics while writing this book, the perennial question was what right do I have to be writing this? In the process of undergoing this book, my methodology and praxis was challenged, especially with regard to the possibilities of existence in liminal spaces. In writing GAZE BACK, I considered new utilities of form and content, breath and space, and was doubly conscious of my social and artistic choices— not least because of the care and incision in Divya's comments, who oversaw the birthing of this manuscript. Moreover, these were framed in contextual terrain that was always highly personal—the local queer scene, the imported Catholicism, the varieties of English I have chosen to feature, the very particular geo-locations mentioned by name. I have had to think closely about what I have been communicating and attempting to disrupt, whether through form (presenting the reader with a flowchart, a grainy picture, a page of programming code) or language.

Ultimately, GAZE BACK is an instruction book, a grimoire, a recipe book; a call to insurrection—to wrest power from the institutionalised social structures that serve to restrict, control and distribute it amongst those whom society values and privileges above the disenfranchised. I hope it discomfits and reassures in equal measure. I hope it is disobedient, difficult, and disarming. And I am grateful for the attention that you have shown it.

'How dangerous can a book be?' This quote was encountered, while writing GAZE BACK, from another poet. I hope to lessen some of the incredulity of that comment.

With special thanks to Professor Divya Victor for her immeasurable guidance and mentorship over the course of a year. She continues to inspire me to be louder, more disobedient, and to gaze back unflinching.